THE BLACK WEALTH CURVE

by

BRIAN B. TURNER

For permissions requests, inquiries, or more information, contact:

Published by HEY BBT LLC
www.heybbt.com

ISBN (Paperback): *978-1-971050-06-5*
ISBN (Hardcover): *978-1-971050-07-2*
ISBN (eBook): *978-1-971050-05-8*

First Edition

Printed in the United States of America

Table of Contents

A NOTE ON THE BLACK WEALTH PAPERS

The Black Wealth Papers began as a question. Why do so many Black families feel behind, even when they are working harder, carrying more, and rising higher than the generations before them?

My book *Why You Are Not Behind* answered part of that question. It reframed individual timelines and exposed the pressure Black families feel when they compare their progress to people who inherited a different starting point.

But individual awareness was only the beginning.

The deeper story lives in history.
In policy.
In access.
In compounding.
In the conditions that shaped Black wealth long before any of us were born.

The Black Wealth Papers exist because these truths were never handed to us. They are the histories, frameworks, and realities that should have been passed down but were not. They are the explanations behind outcomes often mistaken as personal rather than structural.

Each book in the series focuses on a specific part of the curve that shaped Black life in America. Some parts are historical. Some are generational. Some are psychological. All of them reveal the truth behind what we often misunderstand as individual results.

This first volume, *The Black Wealth Curve*, begins with the timeline itself. It explains how the curve was created, where it bent, and why so many Black families start their progress inside a structure they did not choose.

If *Why You Are Not Behind* helped readers understand their personal journey, The Black Wealth Papers exist to show the larger journey their families have been living for generations.

This is the beginning of that work.

INTRODUCTION

The Line Before You

There is a line that runs through every Black family in America.

A line made of choices they never had, opportunities they were denied, and possibilities they were forced to imagine without support. A line shaped long before your birth. A line that explains why some families rose with ease while others climbed without rest. A line that does not appear on any map or chart, yet determines the pace of entire generations.

This book is about that line.

It begins long before you.
It begins with people who carried more than they could ever keep.
It begins in a country that renamed inequality as normal.

Some families inherited time.
Others inherited delay.

Some inherited property.
Others inherited the rent receipts that replaced it.

Some inherited stability.
Others inherited the work it takes to catch up to that stability.

Some families inherit assets.
Others inherit the work it takes to catch up to those assets.

This is the story of the curve beneath those differences. Not the curve of income or behavior, but the curve of history. The curve that shapes who starts with momentum and who starts with memory.

The Grandfather

Picture three men returning home from the same war.

They were drafted at the same age.
They trained on the same fields.
They slept in the same barracks.
They risked their lives under the same sky.

But when the war ended, their futures did not.

One stepped into a world designed to lift him.
One stepped into a world determined to stall him.
One stepped into a world that pretended opportunity was equal.

The first man used the GI Bill to buy a small house on a quiet street, a house that later became the first asset in his family's history. A foundation. A starting point. A door that stayed open.

The second man, also eligible, was turned away by banks, blocked by realtors, rejected by colleges, and told that the benefits he earned were not meant for people who looked like him. He returned home without the bridge that others walked across.

The third man never questioned why the gap grew between them.
He simply accepted the story he was told.
Some people used their opportunities well.
Some did not.

But that was not the truth.

What one man received became the inheritance that lifted his grandchildren.
What one man was denied became the burden his grandchildren carried.

This was the first bend in the curve.

The Parents

Now picture the next generation.

Children growing up in neighborhoods divided by old policies and old lines. Children attending schools funded by property taxes their families never had the chance to build. Children watching their parents work long hours without ever breaking even.

The families on one side of the city taught their children how to manage abundance.
The families on the other side taught their children how to stretch survival.

Not because they lacked wisdom.
Not because they lacked discipline.
But because they were living inside a system where the foundation had already been poured for them.

Time had been compounding for some families for decades.
Time had been standing still for others.

The curve did not start with the child.
It started with the conditions surrounding the child.

You

And then there is you.

You grew up piecing together a story that was never told in full. You heard phrases like work hard, stay focused, rise above, push through. You believed progress was a straight road and success was a matter of effort alone.

You did not see the families who were already ahead because their timeline began earlier.
You did not see the compounding that worked quietly in the background for generations.

You did not see the invisible inheritance some people receive before they earn their first dollar.

All you saw was the distance.
The distance between effort and outcome.
The distance between potential and possibility.
The distance between where you were and where you thought you should be.

So you called it being behind.

But you were not behind.
You were living inside a curve that was made long before you could name it.

This book exists to reveal that curve.

What This Book Will Show You

This is not a book about blame.
This is a book about clarity.

It will show you how wealth was built in America.
It will show you how policies shaped the lives of people who never had a seat at the table.
It will show you how timelines, not talent, explain the gap.
It will show you how the curve created two Americas.
One with compounding.
One without it.

It will show you why first-generation success feels heavy.
Why progress feels slow.
Why stability feels fragile.
Why you carry pressure that others do not recognize?
Why the path forward requires understanding the path behind you.

And it will show you something more important.

There is nothing wrong with you.
There is nothing wrong with your family.
There is nothing wrong with your pace.

You are living inside a curve that was never designed with your ascent in mind, yet you are ascending anyway.

This Is Where the Curve Changes

The Black Wealth Curve is not a verdict.
It is a beginning.

Once you understand the shape of the story you inherited, you can reshape the story you pass on.
You can build a timeline that finally compounds.
You can create the stability your family never had.
You can shift the weight carried by generations.

You can become the moment where the line turns.

Not because you escaped the curve.
But because you learned how to bend it forward.

CHAPTER 1: THE INTERRUPTED TIMELINE

He did not realize the truth until much later, but the story of his life began years before he was born. It began in a moment that did not include him, a decision made by someone he never met, on a street he never walked, inside a system he never voted for.

He was thirteen when he first wondered why his family seemed to start every year at zero. He saw other kids who lived with a different kind of ease. Their parents talked about stocks and savings. His parents talked about bills and timing. Their weekends were filled with trips and lessons. His weekends were filled with errands and responsibilities. Their homes felt like foundations. His home felt like a reset button.

One evening at the kitchen table, he asked his father why it always felt like they were catching up. His father paused for a long time. Not because he did not know the answer, but because he knew the real answer required a history lesson that would break the moment.

So he said the simplest truth he had.

"Our timeline started different."

It was the first time he realized that life does not move at the same pace for every family. Some people begin on a road already paved. Some begin where the pavement ends. Some inherit time. Some inherit delay. Some inherit stability. Others inherit the work required to create stability from scratch.

He would later learn what his father meant. Not from textbooks. Not from lectures. From life. From watching how far effort can take you and how far history can pull you back at the same time. From understanding that the starting point is rarely the place the world believes it is.

Because the Black timeline in America is not a straight road, it is a road interrupted. Not once. Not twice. But generation after generation. Interrupted by laws, access, policy, and wealth gates that opened for some and stayed locked for others. Interrupted by timelines that rewarded one group for simply being early and punished another for being late to a race they were not allowed to enter.

The Interrupted Timeline is not theory. It is reality. It explains why two families can work the same hours, carry the same values, and raise their children with the same hope, yet end up with entirely different results. It explains why progress feels slow even when it is steady. It explains why stability feels fragile even when you earn it. It explains why the pressure to perform sits heavier on those who start their journey with no margin for error.

Timelines matter more than motivation.
They shape what becomes possible.
They influence what becomes normal.
They define what feels achievable.
They decide how long it takes for progress to show up.

For many Black families, the timeline was interrupted before it could ever compound. Before assets could grow. Before savings could stabilize. Before opportunity could pass from one generation to the next.

So this chapter begins with a truth many people never hear.

There is nothing wrong with your pace.
There is something wrong with the timeline you were given.

The rest of this chapter explains what his father could not fit into one sentence.

Understanding that difference changes everything. It shifts the burden. It reframes the path. It reveals the hidden forces that shape the journey long before effort enters the picture. It shows that the question has never been about why Black families are behind. The real question is why the starting line was moved so many times before they could reach it.

This is the story of the interrupted timeline.
How it was created.
How it shaped the curve.
And how understanding it becomes the first step toward changing it.

The Question That Revealed the Curve

Every timeline carries assumptions. Some begin with inheritance. Some begin with access. Some begin with a clean runway. Others begin with a broken path. When his father said their timeline started differently, he was naming the truth that families rarely say aloud. A timeline is not a moment. It is a structure. It determines what each generation can build, protect, and pass down.

A family with a house purchased in 1950 stepped into compounding.
A family blocked from that purchase stepped into repair work.

Two different timelines.
Two different realities.

The Cost of Being Denied Compounding

Compounding needs time.
Wealth needs time.

Stability needs time.
Opportunity needs time.

Once time is interrupted, everything built on it becomes fragile. A family that starts late is not behind by choice. They are behind by design. An interrupted timeline does not delay one person. It delays entire generations.

The absence of a single asset can erase decades. The presence of one can create decades.

That is the quiet math behind the curve.

The Three Curves

The Interrupted Timeline is not one curve. It is three.

1. The Wealth Curve

The assets, equity, and financial compounding a family can pass down.

A family with a home, a policy, or a small investment begins with traction.
A family without them begins with friction.

2. The Opportunity Curve

The education, networks, and access that shape mobility.

One curve includes tutors, internships, mentors, and margin.
The other includes improvisation, adaptation, and survival.

3. The Safety Curve

The margin, stability, and protection that prevent collapse.

One curve has buffers.
One curve has consequences.

Families starting early rise across all three.
Families starting late struggle across all three.
This has nothing to do with effort.
It begins with time.

Why Catch-Up Is Never a Fair Expectation

Catch-up is a race instruction.
But this was never a race with a single starting line.

You cannot catch up to someone who began generations earlier.
You can only begin where your story starts.

When society compares outcomes without comparing timelines, the comparison becomes punishment. Not truth.

The idea of catching up assumes time was equal.
It was not.

How the Interrupted Timeline Shapes You Today

An interrupted timeline does not end with the past.
It becomes the psychology of the present.

It explains why first-generation progress feels heavy.
It explains why stability feels temporary.
It explains why pressure feels personal even when it
is historical.

Understanding the timeline does not excuse the
struggle.
It explains it.

Understanding the timeline is not closure.
It is the beginning of a different curve.

CHAPTER 2: WHEN THE ROAD WAS DIVIDED

He did not know the year, the policy, or the paperwork. He knew the moment. He was nine years old the first time he noticed that the same city could look like two different worlds. His aunt lived on one side of town, his grandmother on the other. The drive between the two took less than fifteen minutes, yet it felt like crossing a border he did not understand.

On one side, the houses sat close together, their roofs patched, their porches worn from years of weather. People gathered outside because the inside felt too small. On the other side, the blocks seemed wider, the streets quieter, the air somehow lighter. Every lawn looked as if someone had cared for it long before he arrived.

He asked his mother why everything changed once they crossed the railroad tracks. She inhaled, exhaled, and said the same quiet truth so many parents use when the real answer is too heavy for a child.

"This part of town had different rules."

He would learn later that rules can shape a life before a life even starts. Rules can lift one family and limit another. Rules can decide who gets access, who gets stability, and who spends generations trying to rebuild what someone else never had to lose.

He would learn that the road was not naturally divided. Someone divided it. Someone drew the lines. Someone decided where opportunity would live and where it would not.

He would learn that maps are not neutral. They are mirrors of power.

He did not know it then, but the road he traveled as a child was already telling a story about the curve that shaped his life.

The rest of this chapter explains what those rules did to the curve.

The Policies That Built Two Americas

A divided road does not begin with choices. It begins with policy.

Lines drawn on maps.
Neighborhoods labeled safe or unsafe.
Blocks marked valuable or expendable.

These were not accidents. They were decisions.

A home loan approved on one side of town and denied on the other.
A school funded in one zip code and starved in the

next.
A family welcomed into a neighborhood, and another quietly pushed out.

Nothing about the divided road was random.
It was intentional structure.

Red Lines, Red Labels, and Red Futures

Redlining was not simply a housing policy. It was a generational sorting system.

A system that said:
This neighborhood deserves investment.
That neighborhood does not.
These families can build equity.
Those families cannot.

A red line on a map became a redirection of futures.

The value of a home determined the value of the schools.
The value of the schools shaped the value of the opportunities.
The value of the opportunities shaped the value of the timeline.

A simple line on a federal map became the first major bend in the Black Wealth Curve.

The Road With the Green Light

On the other side of the line, everything that compounding requires was already present.

Appreciating property.
Stable schools.
Safe neighborhoods.
Predictable costs.
Intergenerational guidance.

Families on this road did not have to start over.
They started ahead.

Not because of effort.
But because of placement.

The Road With the Stop Sign

For Black families, the divided road meant something else entirely.

Rent instead of ownership.
Overcrowded schools instead of funded ones.
Stress instead of stability.
Neighborhoods shaped by extraction rather than investment.

A redlined block was not just a location.
It was a timeline interruption.

Every denied mortgage was a denied inheritance.
Every undervalued home was a stolen decade.

Every forced relocation was a broken link in the chain of compounding.

The wealth curve did not dip by accident.
It was bent by design.

Two Roads, Two Destinies

By the time a single generation passed, the difference between the roads had become a difference between realities.

One road built wealth.
The other built resilience.

One road created margin.
The other created pressure.

One road produced families that could plan.
The other produced families that had to react.

The country told everyone the roads were the same.
But the outcomes told the truth.

What This Division Did to the Curve

The divided road created the first large-scale separation in American financial life. It established the pattern that continues today:

- Where you live shapes what you can build.

- What you can build shapes what you can pass down.

- What you can pass down shapes the curve your children inherit.

The road was not just a metaphor.
It was a mechanism.

A dividing line that splits compounding into two paths.

One rising.
One resetting.

For some families, the curve began with oxygen.
For others, it began with weight.

The Road Still Exists

Policies ended.
Maps faded.
Language softened.

The divide remained.

Mortgage approval rates.
Home appraisal gaps.

School funding formulas.
Neighborhood investment patterns.

They all still reflect the old lines.

The road may not look the same as it did decades ago, but the outcomes prove it never disappeared.

To understand the Black Wealth Curve, you must understand this truth:

The road was divided long before the race began. And the finish lines were never placed at the same distance.

CHAPTER 3: THE GI BILL AND THE TWO AMERICAS

He found the folder by accident.

It was tucked inside a box of old uniforms and medals, a box no one had opened since his grandfather passed. Inside the folder was a stack of neatly folded documents, yellowed at the edges but carefully kept. Military discharge papers, training records, and a photograph of a young man standing tall in his dress blues.

And then he saw it.

A letter with a government seal and a sentence that did not fit the stories he grew up hearing.

"We regret to inform you that your application for a home loan has been denied."

He read it twice, then a third time, as if the words might reorganize themselves into something more reasonable. His grandfather had served with honor. He had completed his duty. He had done everything the country asked of him.

But the country did not keep its promise to him.

No one in the family had ever mentioned this letter. Not his mother. Not his uncles. Not the man himself. It was as if the denial had been quietly folded into the family's story, absorbed without explanation, accepted without a fight because fighting systems that were already built against you felt pointless.

He held that letter and realized something he had never understood:

Some families started their futures with approval. His family started with rejection.

This chapter tells the truth behind that letter. And the truth behind millions just like it.

It explains why one of the greatest wealth-building policies in American history lifted some families into stability while leaving others in the same place they started.
It explains why two veterans could return from the same war and enter two different Americas.
It explains the curve.

The Promise That Built a Nation

The GI Bill was introduced as a reward for service, but it became much more than that. It became the engine of the modern middle class. It offered:

- college education

- low-interest mortgages

- business loans

- unemployment support

- on-ramps into stable careers

It was designed to ensure that no veteran returned home without a path forward.

But what was written on paper and what happened in practice were not the same story.

The federal government created the promise.
Local institutions controlled the access.

Banks.
Universities.
Real estate boards.
Appraisal systems.
Neighborhood associations.

In some cities, fewer than two out of every one hundred Black veterans received the mortgages they were promised, while White veterans were approved by the thousands.

They turned one national policy into two lived realities.

The America That Approved the Letters

For White veterans, the GI Bill became a generational springboard:

A mortgage approved in a growing suburb.
A house purchased at a price that would multiply over the decades.
Entry into neighborhoods that were designed to rise in value.
Access to colleges that opened doors to higher salaries and career mobility.
Stability that their children would inherit before they were old enough to understand its meaning.

One approval letter could create a lifetime of margin.
One house could become a financial foundation.
One degree could elevate every generation that followed.

This was the America where compounding began early and quietly.

This was the America where the curve rose.

The America That Denied Them

Black veterans came home to a different reality:

Loan denials.
Closed doors.
"Lost" paperwork.

Neighborhood restrictions disguised as policy.
Educational opportunities rerouted or fully blocked.

It was not always spoken aloud, and it did not have to be.
The system knew how to produce the same outcome without ever writing it explicitly.

Here is the truth that families rarely say out loud:

Some men did not fail to build wealth.
They were prevented from beginning.

The letter his grandfather received was not a refusal.
It was a redirection away from compounding.
Away from the curve.

Because when a family is blocked from homeownership in 1946, the cost is not one house.
It is eighty years of equity they never had the chance to grow.

When One Policy Creates Two Curves

Two veterans wearing the same uniform could leave the war and enter two realities that never touched.

Curve One: The Pathway Upward

- A house that grows in value

- A neighborhood that appreciates

- Schools with funding

- Degrees that unlock careers

- Children raised with margin

Curve Two: The Pathway Delayed

- Renting with no equity

- Neighborhoods undervalued by design

- Schools underfunded

- Job paths limited to what was accessible, not what was deserved

- Children raised inside the pressure their parents could not escape

This was not about personal effort.
It was about the shape of the starting point.

One curve rose with every decade.
The other had to restart every decade.

The Myth of Equal Reward

For generations, a single myth survived far longer than the truth:

"Everyone who served had the same opportunity afterward."

But veterans did not receive the same approvals.
They did not receive the same neighborhoods.
They did not receive the same educational pathways.
They did not receive the same valuation of their futures.

The myth was comforting.
The truth was dividing.

The GI Bill was equal in theory.
America was not equal in practice.

What We Inherited

A denied benefit in one generation becomes a missing foundation in the next.

Children born into these two realities grew up believing the differences were personal:

Some families seemed more stable.
Some seemed more prepared.
Some seemed to make better decisions.
Some seemed to move ahead faster.

But the truth is simpler:

Some families inherited the runway.
Others inherited the work it takes to reach the
runway.

The letter in that old folder did not deny one man a
house.
It denied a family a curve.

Understanding that is not anger.
It is accuracy.
It is the beginning of reshaping what comes next.

CHAPTER 4: THE MATH THAT NEVER WORKED

He heard the same sentence repeated throughout his childhood: "You just have to be smart with your money."

It came from teachers, neighbors, mentors, and even relatives. It was said with good intentions, the kind spoken as advice but carried as pressure. He believed it for years, until he grew older and realized something no one had ever explained.

Money math is not the same as wealth math.

Money math is the arithmetic of the present. Wealth math is the compounding of the past.

He remembered watching his mother write numbers on the back of an envelope. She tapped the pen twice before writing, a small habit she developed whenever she needed the math to stretch further than the money allowed. Rent, utilities, gas, groceries. She was careful, disciplined, organized. Her math was precise. But no matter how carefully she added and subtracted, the total never created the margin she was aiming for.

It took him years to understand why.

She was balancing today on top of a past that never compounded.

This chapter explains the math that never worked.
Not because Black families miscalculated.
But because they were never allowed to use the same formula.

The Arithmetic of Survival

Most Black families did not grow up calculating investments, appreciation, or compound interest. They calculated:

- How to stretch one check until the next

- How to make rent without falling behind

- How to help extended family without destabilizing their own home

- How to recover from the unexpected with no buffer to absorb the blow

This is survival arithmetic.
It is not mismanagement.
It is mathematics without margin.

You cannot build wealth on arithmetic that begins at zero every month.
You can only maintain stability long enough to try again.

Survival math creates responsible people.
It does not create compounding.

The Math That Requires Time

Wealth math is different.
It requires:

Time.
Patience.
Stability.
The ability to wait for growth instead of chasing recovery.
The ability to invest without the fear that the money will be needed tomorrow.

Wealth math does not reward intelligence alone.
It rewards uninterrupted time.

This is where the curves diverge.

Families who entered the wealth formula early could:

- buy appreciating assets

- wait for market cycles

- leverage equity

- invest from stability instead of urgency

- make long-term decisions without short-term panic

They were not better at math.
They were inside a different equation.

When the Starting Point Distorts the Formula

Two families can use the same financial advice and arrive at opposite outcomes.

One invests extra money into retirement.
The other uses that same money to repair a car that cannot be replaced.

One maxes out contributions because they have margin.
The other puts off contributions because emergencies come first.

One uses equity to buy a second property.
The other uses credit to pay for medical bills.

The formula is not equal when the variables are not equal.

Traditional wealth advice assumes:

- stability

- inheritance

- access

- the absence of systemic setbacks

- a buffer against emergencies

Most Black families were never given those starting variables.

The math did not fail.
The inputs were never the same.

The Invisible Cost of Resetting

The greatest financial burden on Black families has never been spending.
It has been resetting.

Every emergency that wipes out savings.
Every job loss that resets momentum.
Every move caused by rising rent.
Every family obligation that requires stepping in.
Every denied opportunity that forces a new plan.

Resetting interrupts compounding.
It steals time.
It breaks the formula at the point where growth should begin.

Some families build on top of yesterday.
Others must rebuild yesterday before they can start today.

Those curves will never look the same.

The Gap Between Advice and Reality

The financial world loves simple rules:

Save 20 percent.
Invest early.
Buy instead of rent.
Avoid debt.

These rules are true, but they are not universal.

They are written from the vantage point of people who:

- inherited margin

- had support through emergencies

- bought homes early

- gained access to credit without discrimination

- operated inside stable economic environments

Advice assumes a smooth runway.
Reality rarely provides one.

You cannot follow wealth advice designed for families who never had to start over.

The Curve Inside the Equation

When the math does not work, the conclusion is often:

"I must be doing something wrong."

But the truth is mathematical, not moral.

When a family begins with no inherited assets, no margin, no buffer, and no safety net, they must use their income to create stability, not compounding. That is not failure. That is physics.

Compounding wealth requires:

- available capital

- time without interruption

- room for error

- long-term stability

Most Black families were excluded from those prerequisites for generations.

The curve you inherit becomes the math you live inside.

Seeing the Formula Differently

You cannot fix math by blaming the calculator.
You cannot solve for the wrong variable.
You cannot change an equation without acknowledging its original inputs.

Understanding this chapter is not about excuses.
It is about accuracy.

It is the moment you stop judging your progress by formulas that were never designed for your starting point.

Because once you understand why the math never worked in the past, you can begin shaping a curve that will.

The future does not change when the numbers change. It changes when the formula finally belongs to you.

CHAPTER 5: THE GAP THAT WAS MISDIAGNOSED

There is a moment every child remembers, even if they never speak about it.
The moment they first sensed they were being compared.

For him, it happened in fourth grade. His class had been assigned a group project, and the teacher cheerfully paired students based on "similar abilities." He noticed the pattern before anyone else did. He felt his stomach drop in that quiet way children do when they understand something before they can explain it. Some students were grouped with high expectations, given the challenging roles. Others, including him, were assigned the simpler tasks, the ones considered easier to manage.

He remembered looking at the other groups and wondering what silent equation had placed him where he was. He had not done anything wrong. He had not fallen behind. Yet he felt the weight of being measured against a standard that had nothing to do with him.

That was the first time he felt the gap.
Not the real gap.
The diagnosed one.

The rest of this chapter explains why the world misread that gap, how that misreading shaped entire generations, and why the diagnosis was wrong before it was even spoken.

The Story America Told Itself

For decades, society explained the wealth gap using narratives that sounded logical but were built on incomplete frames:

"Some families work harder."
"Some people make better choices."
"Some communities value education more."
"Anyone can make it if they try hard enough."

These sentences became cultural wallpaper, repeated often enough to feel true, yet disconnected from the actual timeline.

They framed the gap as a matter of effort instead of access.
As a matter of discipline instead of design.
And as a matter of personal responsibility, instead of inherited trajectory.

A misdiagnosis repeated long enough becomes accepted truth.

And accepted truth becomes identity.

The Metrics That Never Fit

America loves measurement. It measures:

Grades.
Income.
Test scores.
Savings.
Homeownership rates.
Career advancement.

But measurement only works when both sides begin from the same baseline.

When families enter an equation generations apart, the numbers do not reflect ability or ambition. They reflect the timing of opportunity.

Here is the truth hidden beneath decades of charts and comparisons:

A gap created by policy cannot be closed by personality.
A gap created by exclusion cannot be solved by effort alone.
A gap created by time cannot be judged by speed.

Yet the nation used metrics designed for the advantaged to evaluate the progress of the excluded.

The data was accurate.
The interpretation was not.

The Burden of Visibility

Misdiagnosis does not just distort statistics.
It distorts identity.

Generations of Black children grew up being
praised for "defying the odds."
They were called exceptional. Gifted. Rare.
But even compliments carried a hidden weight.

Why should rising require being exceptional?
Why should stability require outperforming the
starting point by unimaginable margins?
Why should the ordinary milestones of life feel like
miracles?

A system that celebrates you for surviving
conditions it created is not offering praise.
It is offering evidence.

Evidence of the curve.
Evidence of the divide.
Evidence of a misdiagnosed gap interpreted as
personal triumph instead of structural truth.

The Blame That Was Misplaced

When the wrong diagnosis takes root, blame travels in predictable directions.

Some families blamed themselves.
Some blamed their neighborhoods.
Some blamed their children.
Some blamed each other.
Some blamed culture instead of conditions.

The nation blamed everything except the original fracture point.

The misunderstanding was so complete that people began solving for problems that did not cause the gap in the first place.

Budgeting workshops for families who were denied credit.
Discipline lectures for communities blocked from homeownership.
Success stories used as proof that barriers did not exist.
Motivational speeches used to quiet generational wounds.

Effort is necessary.
But effort cannot replace the decades when compounding never began.

You cannot close a structural gap with personal strategies.

What Was Really Missing

The gap that America measured was not:

Income.
Intelligence.
Ambition.
Morality.

The real gap was:

Time.
Margin.
Compounding.
Uninterrupted growth.
Inherited stability.
Access to environments where opportunity was expected, not exceptional.

These are not traits. They are conditions.

Conditions that shape:

- How early a family can buy a home

- How quickly savings grow

- How much risk a person can take

- How strongly networks form

- How easily education translates into opportunity

- how rarely a crisis can erase years of progress

The misdiagnosis happened because America measured outcomes while ignoring the variables.

The Curve Behind the Gap

Misdiagnosis led to a deeper confusion:

People assumed the gap reflected effort.
In reality, the gap reflected distance along the curve.

The curve shaped by:

- exclusion from early wealth policies

- neighborhoods designed to depreciate

- credit systems built to deny

- schooling tied to property value

- work structures that rewarded some and stalled others

Once you understand the curve, the expectations change.
The story changes.
The pressure changes.

You stop wondering why the numbers do not match the effort.
You stop comparing your pace to someone else's timeline.
You stop viewing generational struggle as generational failure.

You begin to see the gap for what it always was: misread, misnamed, and misdiagnosed.

You were never behind the truth. The truth was behind the analysis.

CHAPTER 6: THE CURVE THAT STILL SHAPES US TODAY

He used to believe the past was behind him.
That the weight his parents carried was theirs alone.
That every generation begins with a clean slate.

It took adulthood to realize how untrue that was.

The past is not a memory.
It is a structure.
It builds the floor you start on and the ceiling you must reach.
Even when you move forward, it moves with you.

He felt it the first time he looked for an apartment, when he noticed the pattern of neighborhoods he could afford. He realized he was not choosing an address. He was choosing from options shaped by decisions made long before he was born. He felt it again when he applied for credit and saw the difference a family's financial history makes. He felt it most when he became responsible for others, carrying obligations that families with more margin no longer carry by adulthood.

The curve did not stay in the past.
It followed him into every decision.

This chapter explains why.

The Curve Lives in the Map

Cities still reflect the lines drawn decades ago. Some neighborhoods rise faster than others. Some attract investment before residents ask. Some wait years for improvements that others receive by default.

The curve is visible in:

- Where grocery stores open

- Where property values climb

- Where businesses believe customers exist

- Where transportation is reliable

- Where schools have stable funding

- Where safety is assumed instead of earned

People think they are choosing where to live. Often, they are choosing between options shaped long before they were born.

The curve places limits quietly, and because it is quiet, people assume the limits are natural.

The Curve Lives in Credit and Capital

Credit scores measure more than a person's habits.
They measure the financial history of the
environments they survived.

A late payment caused by a crisis.
An unexpected bill with no support to absorb it.
A medical expense paid on credit because savings
had been used to cover someone else's emergency.

These are not signs of irresponsibility.
They are signs of families functioning without
margin.

Yet credit systems do not measure context.
They measure outcomes.

A lower score becomes a higher cost.
A higher cost becomes a slower climb.
A slower climb becomes a curve that rises at a
different pace than those who began with inherited
stability.

The past becomes present again.

The Curve Lives in Opportunity Timing

People talk about opportunity as if it arrives evenly.
It does not.

Opportunity requires time to prepare.
It requires a buffer that allows risk.
It requires freedom from crises that pull focus and resources away.

Two people can have the same potential but not the same availability.
One can say yes to an opportunity immediately.
The other must stabilize their world first.

Potential does not create opportunity.
Stability does.

The curve determines how long it takes to reach that stability.

The Curve Lives in Family Obligation

In many Black families, progress is not individual.
It is collective.

A child's success becomes support for siblings.
A parent's progress becomes protection for elders.
A single income may stabilize multiple households.

These responsibilities are not burdens.
They are acts of love.

But they shape the curve.

Margin that could have become investment becomes support.
Savings that could have compounded become

recovery.
Dreams that could have been pursued earlier
become delayed.

Some families receive support from generations
before them.
Others become the support for generations behind
them.

Both are forms of strength.
Only one accelerates the curve.

The Curve Lives in the Pace of Progress

Some people move through life with the
expectation of steady growth.

Promotions come right on time.
Raises follow predictable cycles.
Emergencies are rare and manageable.

Others live life in seasons.

A breakthrough followed by a setback.
Momentum followed by interruption.
Progress followed by responsibility.

This is not a lack of discipline.
It is the math of margin.

A curve that rises without interruption looks like
acceleration.
A curve that must restart looks like inconsistency.

But inconsistency is often a symptom of starting farther back with less support.

The Curve Lives in How You See Yourself

The deepest effect of the curve is not financial.
It is psychological.

It shapes:

How you measure your pace.
How you judge your mistakes.
How you interpret delays.
How you understand success.
How you define failure.
How you compare yourself to others who were placed on a different timeline.

You begin to think you are behind.
In reality, you are moving through a landscape someone else designed.

The curve you inherited still shapes:

Your decisions.
Your confidence.
Your opportunities.
Your sense of possibility.
Your interpretation of progress.

Seeing the curve does not erase the work.
It reframes the meaning of the work.

It is the moment you stop blaming yourself for a trajectory that began before your name was ever written on the page.

You are not shaped by the curve to stay within it. You are shaped by it to understand the path you are now capable of changing.

CHAPTER 7: THE COMPOUNDING OF PRESSURE

He used to think pressure came from one direction.
Bills.
Deadlines.
Unexpected expenses.
Moments that demanded quick answers and faster action.

But the older he became, the more he realized that pressure did not arrive as an event.
It arrived as a structure.

He remembered the first time he felt it all at once. He felt a tightness in his chest, the kind that arrives when good news and bad news reach you at the same time and you cannot celebrate one without solving the other. He had just started a new job, one he hoped would finally give him the breathing room he had been working toward. But on the same day he received his first paycheck, he also received three calls.

One from a relative who needed help.
One from his mother, whose car had broken down.
One from a bill he thought he had a little more time to handle.

He stood there with the paycheck in his hand, realizing that progress and pressure had shown up together. He was moving forward, but so were the responsibilities tied to every step.

Pressure, he would learn, compounds just as quietly as wealth does.
The difference is that one builds margin.
The other consumes it.

This chapter explains the curve made of pressure.
The curve that rises even when income does.
The curve that shapes opportunity, pace, and identity long before a single financial decision is made.

Pressure Begins With Responsibility Instead of Resources

In some families, adulthood begins with a cushion.
In others, it begins with a list.

Check on your parents.
Help your siblings.
Support extended family.
Cover emergencies no one else can.
Protect the household from falling behind.
Be the stability the family never had.

These responsibilities are acts of love.
They are also forms of pressure that grow over time.

For many Black families, adulthood does not start at zero.
It starts in the negative.

Not morally.
Mathematically.

You inherit responsibility before you inherit resources.
You inherit expectation before you inherit stability.

Pressure begins accumulating before compounding ever has the chance to start.

Pressure Turns Every Choice Into a Calculation

When pressure mounts, decisions carry weight that other families never feel.

A job is not a job.
It is a lifeline.

A promotion is not advancement.
It is insurance against falling behind.

A setback is not temporary.
It can erase years of progress in a moment.

Every choice becomes a negotiation between what builds your future and what protects your present.
That negotiation shapes the curve.

Pressure changes how you take risks, where you live, what opportunities you can pursue, and how quickly you can move.
Not because you lack ambition.
Because you cannot gamble with stability.

When your margin is thin, even progress requires caution.

Pressure Compounds Through Crisis

Every family experiences crisis.
But crisis means something different when margin is thin.

When a car breaks down in a family with savings, it is an inconvenience.
When a car breaks down in a family without savings, it is an interruption that ripples through employment, childcare, timing, and emotional calm.

For families already managing layered responsibilities, one crisis leads to:

A withdrawal from savings.
A new balance on a credit card.
A missed payment that raises interest.
A delay that triggers a fee.
A fee that triggers another reset.

The emergency ends.
The compounding does not.

Years later, people see the credit score but not the crisis.
They see the interest rate but not the timeline.
They see the debt but not the decade that shaped it.

Pressure Reduces the Ability to Plan

Planning requires space.
Pressure consumes space.

You cannot plan long-term goals when you are solving short-term emergencies.
You cannot invest consistently when your money is required to stabilize others.
You cannot take time to breathe when you are still trying to recover from the last interruption.

This creates a loop.

The absence of planning leads to more pressure.
More pressure leads to more interruptions.
More interruptions lead to more resets.

The curve flattens not because people lack strategy.
It flattens because strategy requires margin.

You cannot build a future while fighting for the present.

Pressure Shapes Identity and Pace

The emotional weight of pressure is often overlooked.

Carrying multiple roles creates:

Hyper-awareness of money
Constant vigilance
Chronic worry
Exhaustion mistaken for lack of discipline
Delay mistaken for inconsistency
Success mistaken for luck

Pressure convinces people that they are behind even when they are moving at a pace that would be exceptional in any other context.

It becomes harder to celebrate progress when pressure absorbs the feeling before you have time to feel it.

You are not behind.
You are carrying more than the curve ever measured.

When Pressure Becomes the Default Setting

Generational pressure becomes normalized.
It becomes the background noise of adulthood.
It becomes the expectation placed on the most capable person in the family.

But pressure that compounds becomes a curve of its own:

- It slows advancement even as effort increases

- It delays the moment where compounding can begin

- It magnifies risk and consequences

- It shapes how confidently you move

- It influences every opportunity you say yes or no to

This curve explains why two people with equal potential can have entirely different trajectories.
One is building.
The other is building while holding.

Both are strong.
Only one is measured accurately.

Understanding Pressure Changes the Story

Pressure should not be romanticized.
It should be recognized.

When you understand the compounding effect of pressure, you see:

Why some people seem tired even when they are moving forward.
Why some victories feel smaller than they should.
Why some delays are not signs of weakness but signs of responsibility.
Why your pace is not a reflection of your potential.

Pressure is part of the curve.
But it is not the end of the curve.

Seeing it clearly is the beginning of changing the direction it points you toward.

Pressure may shape the pace, but it never defines the destination.

CHAPTER 8: THE WEALTH THAT COULD NOT BE SEEN

He once believed wealth meant what he could hold in his hand.

He remembered the first time that belief cracked, a quiet afternoon when he noticed how much strength lived in the people around him, even when money did not.

What he could deposit.
What he could purchase.
What he could measure.

But as he grew older, he began noticing something else: a kind of wealth that lived in his family long before anyone earned a dollar.

He saw it when his grandmother cooked enough for anyone who walked through the door.
He saw it when neighbors checked on each other, even when they were struggling themselves.
He saw it in the late-night conversations where stories of survival were passed down like inheritance.
He saw it in the way his mother never let a crisis erase her calm, as if steadiness itself was a resource she had learned to multiply.

It was a wealth that did not show up on paper. It shaped every person who came out of that house.

There was wealth here.
It simply was not recognized as wealth.

This chapter explains the forms of wealth the world overlooked, the ones that kept families afloat when the economic curve was not in their favor, and the ones that must be acknowledged if the full story of progress is ever to be told.

The Wealth of Resilience

Resilience is a currency.
It is earned, not inherited.
It carries interest through difficulty and returns strength in moments that should break a person.

Black families mastered resilience because history demanded it.
But resilience became so normal that it stopped being valued.

Resilience does not raise credit scores.
It does not lower interest rates.
It does not qualify as collateral.

Yet resilience creates something far more powerful.
It creates the ability to continue.

In a world built on interruptions, the ability to continue is a form of wealth.

The Wealth of Support Networks

Many Black families built networks long before the word network became fashionable.

A cousin who watches your children.
A neighbor who shares food when money is tight.
A friend who protects you when the world becomes dangerous.
A community that steps in when a government does not.

These networks reduce isolation.
They reduce risk.
They reduce collapse.
They reduce the emotional stress of navigating systems not designed with your survival in mind.

Support does not show up in an economic report.
But without it, progress would not have been possible.

The Wealth of Cultural Capital

Cultural capital is the knowledge you inherit from the people who raised you.

It includes:

How to read a room
How to spot danger
How to negotiate unspoken rules
How to carry yourself with dignity in spaces
designed to misread you
How to survive without losing your identity

This capital is not taught in classrooms.
It does not earn diplomas.
It does not receive awards.

But it protects.
It guides.
It strengthens.
It gives children tools their parents never had
names for.

It is wealth handed down through experience
instead of assets.

The Wealth of Creativity and Adaptability

When you grow up with fewer resources, you learn
to solve problems with imagination.

Creativity becomes strategy.
Adaptability becomes intelligence.
Improvisation becomes planning.

These are not substitutes for wealth.
They are responses to the absence of wealth.

But responses can also be forms of power.

Creativity turns limits into workarounds.
Adaptability turns obstacles into routes.
Improvisation turns pressure into possibility.

Some families built their futures not by following
instructions but by inventing solutions.

That is wealth the world did not count.

The Wealth of Identity and Story

There is a form of wealth in knowing who you are.

In knowing where you come from.
In knowing the resilience of your lineage.
In learning your family's untold stories.
In carrying history as pride instead of burden.

Identity is a compass.
It gives direction when opportunity is unclear.
It gives confidence when the world mismeasures
your worth.
It gives grounding when the curve feels unfair.

This, too, is wealth.

Not the kind that compounds in a bank.
The kind that compounds in the mind.

Why Invisible Wealth Matters

Invisible wealth does not replace financial wealth. It prepares people to survive the absence of it.

For generations, Black families succeeded not because the curve was fair, but because they developed forms of wealth the country did not recognize.

Invisible wealth:

- Carried families through hardship

- Built character in the face of inequity

- Created communities that protected one another

- Preserved identity when systems attempted to erase it

- Ensured that children believed in their futures even when society did not

Invisible wealth may not have built assets.
But it built people.

And people built the future.

The Curve and the Invisible Ledger

The curve that shaped Black families was not only economic.
It was emotional.
It was cultural.
It was communal.
It was psychological.

The world measured the wrong ledger.

It counted income and ignored resilience.
It counted assets and ignored sacrifice.
It counted opportunity and ignored ingenuity.
It counted financial inheritance and ignored cultural inheritance.

To understand the Black wealth story, you must see both ledgers.
The visible and the invisible.
The measurable and the lived.
The financial and the human.

Wealth is not only what you pass down.
It is what you pass on.

And what was passed on kept the curve alive, even when the numbers said it should have broken.

Invisible wealth may not have built the world they entered, but it shaped the strength they carried into the one they are building now.

CHAPTER 9: THE SLOW WORK OF PROGRESS

He used to believe progress would feel loud.
He thought it would arrive with announcements
and celebrations, with conversations that made it
clear something had changed.
But progress in his family did not look like that.

It looked like his mother keeping the lights on even
when the bills stacked higher than the hours she
had left in the day.
It looked like his grandmother stretching food to
feed more people than the recipe claimed it could
serve.
It looked like his older cousins finding ways to
protect him from mistakes they had already learned
the hard way.
It looked like survival carrying itself one inch further
than the moment before.

None of it looked like winning.
But all of it was progress.

He did not understand that at first.
Most people do not.
We mistake noise for movement and speed for
advancement.
We forget that before progress becomes visible, it
must first become possible.

This chapter is about the progress that did not show up in photos, charts, celebrations, or bank accounts. The progress that happens in the shadows of work, trial, and exhaustion.
The progress that came from families who were doing everything they could to give the next generation a gentler starting point than the one they received.

It is the slow work of progress, and it is the real beginning of any curve that rises.

Progress Is Often a Repair, Not a Leap

For many Black families, the earliest form of progress was not a jump forward.
It was an attempt to fix what history broke.
Repairing takes time.
Rebuilding takes longer.

Before a family can move up, it often must heal from what pulled it down.

Healing does not accelerate the curve, but it removes the weight that kept the curve from rising.

That healing is not linear.
It is not glamorous.
It does not announce itself.

But when a generation silently shoulders burdens the next one will not have to carry, that is progress.

They repaired the timeline even when they could
not accelerate it.

Progress Happens in the Margins

Not every form of progress lives in the center of a
family's story.
Sometimes it happens in the margins:

Paying off a small debt.
Finishing a certification.
Choosing a safer neighborhood.
Leaving a harmful relationship.
Saying no to one more crisis.

None of these moments feel monumental.
But each one bends the curve.

Progress is not a single decision.
It is the accumulation of better margins.

One Generation Pushes, the Next One Starts

This truth is difficult but necessary:

The generation that pushes the hardest rarely
enjoys the outcome.

Their role is to create conditions.
To clear space.
To open doors.

To remove barriers so the next generation finally begins at zero instead of negative ten.

Progress is not immediate.
It is inherited.
And sometimes the greatest gift one generation gives is the freedom for the next to move without the weight they carried.

The Curve Moves Slowly, Then All at Once

Progress rarely looks dramatic while it is happening.
It looks repetitive.
It looks exhausting.
It looks like nothing is changing.

But slow does not mean stagnant.

A curve rises gradually until it hits a point where the upward shift becomes visible.
The family that has been investing in stability for decades finally sees what that stability makes possible.

It is the moment when consistency becomes momentum.
The moment when survival becomes strategy.
The moment when the slow work reveals its speed.

The Misunderstanding of "Not Far Enough"

People often compare their lives to others who had uninterrupted compounding.
They forget they are comparing their chapter three to someone else's chapter twelve.

Progress cannot be measured by pace.
It can only be measured by direction.

If the curve is no longer declining, that is progress.
If the collapse has stopped, that is progress.
If the next generation starts with fewer wounds and more tools, that is progress.

Progress is not only how far you move.
It is everything you did not have to relive.

The Honor in Slow Progress

There is dignity in the slow work.
There is legacy in it.
There is unspoken courage in the generations who kept going even when the world misread their progress as failure.

Slow progress is still progress.
Measured progress is still movement.
Invisible progress is still a contribution.

The curve rises because of those who carried weight they never complained about.
Who endured seasons that were not gentle.
Who believed in futures they might not live to see.

These were the builders of the curve.
Their progress was slow.
Their impact was not.

Progress may move slowly, but it always moves in
the direction of the people who refuse to stop.

CHAPTER 10: IDENTITY BEFORE INCOME

He used to believe income would change
everything.
The stress.
The pressure.
The uncertainty.
The feeling of being behind.

But the first time his income finally rose, he noticed
something unsettling.
He stared at the higher number on the screen and
felt his shoulders tense the same way they did when
he was bracing for bad news.
The fear did not fall.
The pressure did not fade.
The worry did not leave.

More money arrived, but the story he carried about
himself stayed the same.

That was the moment he realized something he
had never been taught.
Your income can change without your identity
changing.
And if your identity stays the same, the curve does
too.

This chapter is about the part of the Black wealth
story that almost never gets measured.

The internal world.
The stories families inherit.
The beliefs passed down quietly.
The unspoken lessons that shape confidence, risk tolerance, self-worth, and pace.

This is not psychology for the sake of psychology.
This is the economic truth that many people discover too late.

Identity moves before income does.
And if identity is shaped by interruption, then identity must be repaired before income can rise in a way that sustains.

Identity Begins With What You Saw, Not What You Earn

Children learn wealth long before they learn numbers.
Not through money, but through patterns.

They notice who pays the bills.
Who worries at the table.
Who argues over debt.
Who stays calm through a crisis.
Who dreams out loud and who never gets the chance.

These moments become the blueprint.

If all you saw was survival, identity forms around survival.
If all you saw was repair, identity forms around repair.
If all you saw was interruption, identity forms around interruption.

Identity does not begin with income.
Identity begins with exposure.
And exposure shapes expectation.

A person cannot aim for a curve they have never seen.

Identity Determines Financial Behavior

People do not spend based on income.
They spend based on identity.

Identity affects:

What feels safe
What feels possible
What feels out of reach
What feels too risky
What feels like a threat
What feels like a breakthrough

Two people can earn the same paycheck, but their decisions will be entirely different.

One sees money as a tool for freedom.
The other sees money as a shield against crisis.

One invests early because they trust the future.
The other delays because the future never felt
guaranteed.

One takes risks because the ground beneath them
feels steady.
The other hesitates because the ground has
collapsed before.

Identity directs money long before money directs
identity.

Identity Can Carry Inherited Limits

Families do not just pass down assets.
They pass down beliefs.

Some of the most common inherited identities
include:

The one who must hold the family together
The one who is responsible for everyone
The one who cannot fail because too many people
depend on them
The one who always has to start over
The one who does not deserve ease
The one who should play it safe
The one who must not disappoint
The one who is afraid to dream too loudly

These identities are not weaknesses.
They are survival roles.
They formed in homes where someone had to be
the stability the system refused to provide.

But survival identities do not build wealth.
They protect.
They conserve.
They endure.
They do not expand.

Wealth requires a different identity than the one
created by a life of repair.

Income Cannot Fix an Identity That Was Built in Emergency Mode

When a person grows up in survival, their mind
learns to predict what can go wrong.
It trains itself to anticipate collapse.
It braces even when nothing is falling.

This creates a paradox.
As income rises, fear can rise too.

Not because the person is careless or uneducated.
But because the nervous system remembers what
the numbers tried to forget.

Income cannot overwrite an identity shaped by
instability.

It can only expose the places where identity has not yet healed.

This is why many people finally earn more and still feel behind.
The curve outside them rose.
The curve inside them did not.

Reclaiming Identity Is the Turning Point of the Curve

The moment a person realizes their identity was shaped by interruption, not inadequacy, something shifts.

The shame falls.
The hesitation loosens.
The pressure feels lighter.
The story becomes clearer.

Identity repair is not emotional fluff.
It is economic infrastructure.

When identity changes, behavior changes.
When behavior changes, decisions change.
When decisions change, the curve rises.

The most powerful shift a person can make is not financial.
It is internal.

Identity Before Income Is the New Rule of Progress

Before you judge your pace, ask:

What identity did I inherit
What identity did I build to survive
What identity do I still carry, even though my circumstances have changed
What identity do I need to build now

The curve changes only when the identity behind it changes.

Because the truth is simple.

Income expands opportunity.
Identity determines whether you can take it.

Identity rises first.
Income follows.
The curve shifts after both align.

Identity is the first curve you must correct if you want the next one to rise.

CHAPTER 11: BUILDING WITHOUT INHERITED INSTRUCTIONS

He used to believe that adulthood came with a manual.
He assumed that when he reached a certain age, someone would hand him the blueprint.
The roadmap.
The guidance.
The step-by-step explanation of how life was supposed to work.

He remembered turning twenty-five and waiting for that moment, only to realize no one was coming with the instructions he needed.

But when the moment finally came, there was no manual waiting.
There was no blueprint.
There was no collective memory to lean on or playbook to follow.
There was only motion, guessing, adjusting, and learning through impact.

He realized he belonged to a generation that had to build without inherited instructions.
A generation that was not continuing a family strategy but creating one.

A generation that had to become the architects of a future no one had drawn.

This chapter is about what it means to construct a life while also constructing the foundation that future generations will stand on.
It is the weight of being the first.
The burden of having no template.
And the quiet brilliance of building while still learning how to build.

The Blueprint Many Families Never Received

Some families inherit a financial playbook.
Others inherit a history of surviving without one.

For many Black families, the instructions for:

How to buy a home
How to manage credit
How to invest early
How to scale income
How to negotiate salaries
How to build a safety net

were simply not passed down, not because the elders lacked wisdom, but because the systems they lived in offered them no access to the opportunities these instructions require.

You cannot pass down what you were never allowed to learn.
You cannot teach what no one taught you.

The absence of guidance was not a failure of the family.
It was the result of a system where opportunity arrived late and unevenly.

The First Generation Learns Everything in Real Time

When you do not inherit instructions, you learn by collision.

You learn budgeting after the first overdraft.
You learn credit the moment a denial letter arrives.
You learn negotiation after realizing you accepted far less than your labor was worth.
You learn about emergency funds the day you have none.
You learn the importance of insurance after discovering what happens without it.

Each lesson is earned.
Each mistake is expensive.
Each discovery becomes a blueprint you wish someone had handed you earlier.

And still, you move forward.

Because the first generation does not quit.
It learns, adjusts, repeats, and begins again.

The Identity Burden of Being First

Being first comes with a pressure that is rarely
acknowledged.

You are expected to succeed without a model.
You are expected to break cycles you did not start.
You are expected to build a foundation while
standing on unstable ground.
You are expected to create options for others while
still trying to create them for yourself.

It is not just financial work.
It is emotional labor.
It is mental endurance.
It is a constant negotiation between who you want
to become and the limits you inherited.

You grow while also holding together the pieces of a
world you did not build but still feel responsible for
improving.

And still, the first generation keeps going.
Not because it is easy, but because someone has to
redraw the map.

The First Generation Rewrites the Family Curve

Every family has a curve.
When someone decides to rise above the pattern,
that person becomes the pivot point.

The first generation:

interrupts the decline
stops the resets
creates stability
builds margin
changes expectations
models new behavior

These changes may not look dramatic, but they
alter the entire trajectory.
What took the first generation years to learn
becomes a simple conversation for the next.

Their sacrifice becomes someone else's starting
point.

The Weight of Building While Carrying Others

The first generation rarely travels alone.
It carries parents who never had financial ease.
It carries siblings who are still navigating instability.
It carries younger relatives who watch and model
what they see.
It carries expectations, pressure, and the unspoken
request to be the one who succeeds.

This weight does not mean weakness.
It means responsibility expanded before resources did.

The first generation does not just build its own life.
It becomes the blueprint for the entire family line.

And blueprints built under pressure become the designs future generations depend on.

The Quiet Power of Becoming the Instructions

The irony of the first generation is simple.
You begin without guidance, but if you keep going, you become the guidance.

You become the one who knows how credit works.
You become the one who can explain homeownership.
You become the one who understands saving, investing, negotiating, and planning.
You become the one who ensures the next generation will not start from zero.

You become the instructions your family never had.

This is not just progress.
This is transformation.

The curve changes because you learned what no one could teach you and passed it down so others would not have to learn the same lessons the same way.

The first generation carries the burden of building. The generations after carry the benefit of beginning.

The first generation does not just start the curve. It changes the direction of every curve that follows.

CHAPTER 12: THE FIVE LEVERS OF MODERN WEALTH

He once believed wealth was built by doing more of what previous generations did.
Work harder.
Save more.
Be disciplined.
Stay consistent.

He remembered sitting at his desk one night, exhausted after another twelve-hour day, wondering why doing more was still not moving him forward.

But as he stepped deeper into adulthood, he realized the rules had changed.
The economy had changed.
Technology had changed.
Access had changed.
The pace of opportunity had changed.

The old blueprint was not only outdated.
It was incomplete.

Wealth in this era was no longer built by repeating what earlier generations were taught.
It was built by understanding the modern levers that move money, opportunity, and access at a

speed previous generations could not have imagined.

This chapter explains those levers, not as tactics, but as frameworks.
Frameworks that allow the first generation to move with clarity instead of confusion, with precision instead of overwhelm, and with strategy instead of survival.

Modern wealth is not about luck or timing.
It is about alignment with the five forces that shape opportunity today.

Lever 1: Skills That Compound

In previous generations, income rose through tenure.
The longer you worked, the more you earned.

Today, income rises through skill.
Not through how long you have been working, but through how quickly you learn, update, and adapt.

Compound skills include:

Skills that grow in value over time
Skills that open multiple income paths
Skills that can be transferred to new industries
Skills connected to technology
Skills that scale without increasing labor

These are not random talents.
They are assets that appreciate the way investments do.

The person who commits to skill compounding outpaces the person who relies on time.
The curve rises faster for the one whose learning compounds.

Lever 2: Networks That Multiply Value

For generations, Black families built strength through community.
But modern wealth requires an additional layer: networks that multiply opportunity.

A network is not a group of people you know.
A network is a group of people who create openings you cannot create alone.

Networks offer:

Information you did not have
Options you did not know existed
Access to people who make decisions
Introductions money cannot buy
Advancement you cannot accelerate alone

In a world shaped by proximity, the network is a lever that doubles or triples the impact of skill.

A strong network compresses time.
It collapses delays.
It accelerates the curve.

Lever 3: Technology That Scales Effort

This is the first generation with tools that expand output without expanding exhaustion.

Technology now functions as:

A second brain
A second set of hands
A second source of income
A second pathway to opportunity

Automation, artificial intelligence, digital platforms, distribution systems, and online marketplaces allow people to do in one year what used to take a decade.

This does not replace effort.
It multiplies effort.

Those who adopt technology rise faster than those who rely on manual speed alone.

Technology is not a luxury.
It is leverage.

Lever 4: Ownership That Outlives Labor

For decades, wealth was tied almost entirely to employment.
A job, a salary, a pension.

But the modern curve rises through ownership:

Ownership of ideas
Ownership of platforms
Ownership of equity
Ownership of property
Ownership of digital products
Ownership of intellectual property
Ownership of assets that generate income without additional labor

Ownership is not immediate.
It begins slowly.
But when ownership compounds, it shifts the curve for every generation that follows.

Ownership is the difference between income that stops when you stop working and income that continues even while you rest.

Lever 5: Margin That Creates Opportunity

The most overlooked lever of modern wealth is margin.

Margin in time
Margin in money

Margin in mental space
Margin in emotional clarity

Margin allows people to think instead of react.
Invest instead of panic.
Plan instead of scramble.
Take risks instead of retreat.

Without margin, every emergency becomes a
setback.
With margin, every opportunity becomes a
possibility.

Margin is not the reward of wealth.
It is the foundation of wealth.
 It is the space where the curve begins to rise.

Why These Levers Matter for the First Generation

The first generation does not rise by luck or by
intensity.
It rises by shifting from survival levers to modern
wealth levers.

In survival, the questions are:

What bill must be paid next
What crisis must be solved
What pressure must be handled
What responsibility cannot be delayed

Survival creates urgency, but urgency cannot create elevation

In wealth, the questions become:

What skill can I compound
What network can I build
What technology can I use
What ownership can I gain
What margin can I create

The shift between these two sets of questions is not small.
It is generational.
It is the difference between a life spent repairing and a life spent rising.

The Curve of Modern Wealth Is Not Linear

Modern wealth is not built by one lever alone.
It is built by the interaction between all five.

Each lever increases the power of the others:

Skill amplifies network.
Network accelerates ownership.
Ownership increases margin.
Margin increases capacity for learning.
Technology multiplies everything.

This is how momentum forms.
This is how the curve rises.

This is how the first generation moves from surviving to building.

The curve does not rise through effort alone. It rises through leverage.

And the five levers are the tools that ensure the next part of your curve looks nothing like the beginning.

The future does not rise from effort alone. It rises from the leverage you choose to build.

CHAPTER 13: THE SECOND GENERATIONAL CURVE

He did not notice the moment the curve shifted.
It did not happen in a dramatic announcement, or a sudden breakthrough, or a moment where everything finally made sense.
It happened quietly, almost invisibly, in the small ways life began to feel different.

There was a day when he paid a bill without panic.
A day when he made a decision without fear.
A day when the future felt less like a burden and more like an open space he could actually step into.

These were not victories anyone would celebrate.
But they were signals.
Signals that the curve he inherited was no longer the curve he was passing on.

It felt strange to realize that a single calm moment in his life was something generations before him never had the room to feel.

This chapter is about that shift.
The moment when a person becomes the pivot point for their entire family line.
The moment when the second generational curve begins.

The First Curve Is Survival. The Second Curve Is Direction.

Every family begins its modern story on a first curve shaped by:

Interruption
Pressure
Delayed access
Limited options
Inherited responsibility
Restricted opportunity

The first curve is defined by survival.
It bends around obstacles that should not have been there.
It rises slowly because the ground beneath it was uneven from the start.

But once survival becomes stability, something else becomes possible.
A second curve.

The second curve begins not when survival ends, but when survival stops being the only story.

Direction replaces reaction.
Vision replaces repair.
Purpose replaces urgency.

The second curve is built by the first generation to stand on level ground.

The Second Curve Begins With Choice, Not Chance

On the first curve, a person takes the opportunities they can reach.
On the second curve, they begin to choose.

Choice is generational power.
It reflects a reality where options finally exist, where decisions are not shaped by fear, where the ground is solid enough to stand still before stepping forward.

Choice is:

The ability to think long-term
The ability to refuse certain patterns
The ability to pursue growth instead of escape
The ability to build without the shadow of collapse
The ability to create instead of recover

The second curve forms the moment a person realizes they do not have to repeat the urgency they inherited.

The Second Curve Is Built on Time Instead of Tension

On the first curve, every decision is shaped by tension.

Time feels scarce.
Money feels fragile.
Opportunity feels unpredictable.
Crisis feels inevitable.

But once stability forms, even in small ways, time begins to feel different.

Time becomes a resource instead of a threat.
Time becomes a space for planning instead of reacting.
Time becomes an asset instead of an enemy.

This change in the experience of time is one of the clearest signs that the second curve has begun.

The person is no longer living inside the unpredictable rhythm of interruption.
They are living inside the steadier rhythm of intention.

The Second Curve Expands What the Next Generation Can Expect

Expectation is inheritance.

Children born into the second curve grow up with:

Different assumptions
Different exposures
Different sense of possibility
Different norms around planning

Different understanding of stability
Different relationship with opportunity

They see things the first curve could not show them.

They normalize things the first curve had to fight for.

They begin where the prior generation arrived after years of learning, repairing, and restarting.

The gap between expectation and experience becomes smaller.
The curve becomes smoother.
The path becomes clearer.

This is not entitlement.
It is alignment.

The Second Curve Changes What a Family Believes About Itself

The deepest shift of the second curve is not financial.
It is psychological.

The story inside the family changes.

Instead of:

We are behind
We always struggle
We cannot get ahead

We are trying to survive
We never catch a break

the family becomes anchored in a different internal
narrative.

We build
We plan
We prepare
We invest
We rise

The story changes long before the outcomes do.
And once the story changes, the curve follows.

A family that sees itself as capable begins to act like
it is.

The Second Curve Is the Proof of the First Generation's Work

The first generation often doubts its impact.
They feel the weight of how far they still need to go,
not realizing that the second curve is forming
beneath their feet.

They see the struggle, not the shift.
They see the distance left, not the distance covered.
They see the pressure, not the pivot.

But the second curve is not built loudly.
It is built through:

The bill paid on time
The opportunity taken
The fear faced
The lesson learned
The step not repeated
The boundary set
The plan made
The margin created

The second curve is the evidence that all the quiet work mattered.

It is the generational confirmation that the curve can rise again.

The second curve is the moment a family realizes that what once felt impossible has quietly become its new beginning.

THE BEGINNING OF THE NEXT CURVE

The curve does not end here.
It never did.
Every chapter in this book has been about how the past shaped you, but this one is about how the future answers to you.

There is a point in every family line where someone becomes the hinge.
Not the hero.
Not the exception.
The hinge.
The quiet pivot that turns decades of inherited limitation into decades of expanded possibility.

Most people never realize when they become that person.
It is powerful, but it is also heavy, because the work of turning a curve often begins with carrying what others never had the strength or space to name.
It does not feel grand.
It does not feel cinematic.
It feels like learning something your parents never had the chance to understand.
It feels like seeing something your grandparents were never allowed to see.
It feels like choosing the step they never had the option to take.

That is the beginning of the next curve.

Where the Past Meets the Future

The first curve was built on survival.
It was shaped by policies that interrupted progress,
systems that redirected opportunity, and timelines
that were never designed with your family in mind.

The second curve begins when you understand that
history, not as blame, but as context.
Context is clarity.
Clarity is strategy.

The next curve builds itself in the space that opens
once truth replaces confusion.
When you see how the story started, you finally
understand how to write what comes next.

The truth does not limit you.
The truth positions you.

The Future Responds to the Choices You Make Now

The next curve is not built by luck.
It is built by choice.

The choice to invest earlier than your parents could.
The choice to protect the money your grandparents
never had the luxury to save.

The choice to build credit, ownership, structure, and long-term thinking.
The choice to repair the places where the first curve bent.
The choice to build the places the first curve never reached.

Every choice made with intention becomes a line that future generations will walk on without thinking twice.

This is how the next curve rises.

Your Curve Will Never Look Like Theirs, and That Is Power

The world will try to measure your progress against curves that were never comparable to yours.
But now you understand something different.

You are not late.
You are early.
Early in a timeline your family was never supposed to reach.
Early in the work of rebuilding generational structure.
Early in the knowledge that the curve is not defined by effort, but by access, time, and continuity.

The moment you stop comparing your curve to someone else's, you reclaim the momentum that was already yours.

Your Family Will Start Where You Arrive

What you build is not only for you.
It is for the child who grows up believing stability is normal.
It is for the teenager who learns to expect opportunity instead of fearing collapse.
It is for the adult who will one day make decisions from a place of strategy instead of survival.

The next curve begins the moment your ceiling becomes someone else's floor.

Generational progress does not happen when everything is fixed.
It happens when one person changes the direction of the story.

That person is you.

This Is Where Your Curve Turns Upward

The beginning of the next curve does not ask for perfection.
It asks for awareness.
It asks for intention.
It asks for the kind of quiet decisions that do not look significant today but will become the reason someone in your family grows up believing the world is wider than you did.

Your timeline shifts here.
Your trajectory shifts here.
Your family history shifts here.

This is the beginning of the next curve.
You began this journey trying to understand the curve you inherited. You end it by shaping the one your family will inherit from you.
And you are the one bending it upward.

AUTHOR'S NOTE

I did not sit down to write this book because I wanted to explain economics.
I wrote it because I needed to explain a feeling.
A feeling I carried for years without having the language to describe it.
The quiet pressure.
The invisible comparison.
The sense that no matter how hard I worked, I was still entering the race late.

It took time for me to understand that I was not behind.
I was simply born into a curve I did not create.
A curve shaped long before my story began.

Why You Are Not Behind was the first time I ever talked openly about that curve.
Readers sent messages saying the book finally helped them understand why their progress did not look like the timelines they were taught to admire.
They saw themselves in the breaks, the restarts, the interruptions.
They felt validated, not judged.

It showed me that people were not lacking effort.
They were lacking language for the forces that shaped their starting line

That response made one thing clear.
This was not a single book.

This was a series of conversations that had never been written down with honesty, clarity, or cultural respect.

The Black Wealth Papers was born from that realization.

This volume, *The Black Wealth Curve*, is the foundation.
It explains the forces that shaped our starting line.
It honors the generations who survived what they could not control.
It gives language to stories that were passed down but never documented.
It shows why progress in our community has always required more than effort.
It has required context.
It has required truth.
It has required us.

If you see yourself in these pages, it is because this book was written for the questions you were never given the tools to ask.
Questions about inheritance.
Questions about interruptions.
Questions about why your journey has always felt heavier than the narratives you were compared to.

My hope is that this book does more than explain what happened.
I want it to restore the confidence that history tried to remove.
I want it to give you clarity about where you stand

and what you are building.

I want it to remind you that the curve is rising, even when it feels slow, and that you are not the end of the story.

You are the inflection point.

Thank you for reading.

Thank you for doing the work your ancestors never had the freedom, time, or access to do.

Thank you for becoming the beginning of a curve that bends upward.

This series exists to give us the clarity that history never offered and the language our families were never handed.

This is only the first chapter of the Black Wealth Papers.

There is more to uncover, more to unlearn, and more to build.

The story continues from here.

ACKNOWLEDGMENTS

This book was not created in isolation.
It is the product of years of conversations, quiet observations, family history, cultural memory, and the voices of people who shaped how I see the world.

To my family.
Thank you for being the first curve I ever studied, even when none of us had the language for it.
Your stories, your sacrifices, your resilience, and your contradictions gave me the foundation I needed to write this book with honesty and care.
Everything I understand about inheritance began with you.

To the generations before us who carried more than they could name.
Thank you for surviving what you were never supported to overcome.
Your lives are the reason this book exists.
You held the weight so we could hold the pen.

To everyone who read *Why You Are Not Behind* and reached out to share how it reshaped the way you understood your timeline.
You confirmed that these conversations were not niche.
They were necessary.
Your messages turned one book into a series.

To the readers of this book.
Thank you for approaching these pages with an open mind and a willingness to see your story differently.
Thank you for your honesty, your vulnerability, and your desire to understand where you truly stand in the larger arc of history.

To the people who trusted me with their experiences, their frustrations, and the unspoken questions they carried about money, progress, and family.
This book carries pieces of those conversations.
Your transparency helped me build this work with clarity and depth.

To my children.
You are the reason I care so deeply about the curves we inherit and the curves we build.
Everything I write is shaped by the future I want you to walk into.
You deserve a world where the starting line is not something you must fight to redefine.

To the readers who are carrying stories that were never fully explained to them, thank you for choosing to understand your curve instead of accepting the version the world handed you.

And finally, to every person who is the first in their family to face the weight of change.
The ones repairing timelines they did not break.
The ones building stability they never saw.

The ones carrying expectations they never asked for.
Thank you for your strength.
Thank you for your courage.
Thank you for being the hinge that turns the curve upward.

This book is for you.
The next curve begins with you.

www.ingramcontent.com/pod-product-compliance
Lightning Source LLC
Chambersburg PA
CBHW021624270326
41931CB00008B/849